Horses!

Working Horses

Patricia K. Kummer

Cavendish
Square

New York

Published in 2014 by Cavendish Square Publishing, LLC
303 Park Avenue South, Suite 1247, New York, NY 10010

Website: cavendishsq.com

This publication represents the opinions and views of the author based on his or her personal experience, knowledge, and research. The information in this book serves as a general guide only. The author and publisher have used their best efforts in preparing this book and disclaim liability rising directly or indirectly from the use and application of this book.

CPSIA Compliance Information: Batch #WS13CSQ

All websites were available and accurate when this book was sent to press.

Library of Congress Cataloging-in-Publication Data
Kummer, Patricia K.
Working horses / Patricia K. Kummer
        p. cm. — (Horses!)
Includes bibliographical references and index.
Summary: "Provides comprehensive information on working horses"—Provided by publisher
ISBN 978-1-60870-840-6 (hardcover)   ISBN 978-1-62712-090-6 (paperback)   ISBN 978-1-60870-846-8 (ebook)
1. Draft horses—Juvenile literature. 2. Horses—Juvenile literature. 3. Working animals—Juvenile literature. I. Title.
SF311.K86 2013
636.1'5—dc23
2011029916

Editor: Christine Florie
Art Director: Anahid Hamparian
Series Designer: Virginia Pope

Expert Reader: Carissa Wickens, assistant professor, Equine Extension Specialist, University of Delaware, Department of Animal and Food Sciences, Newark, Delaware

Photo research by Marybeth Kavanagh

Cover photo by Johan De Meester/Ardea.com

The photographs in this book are used by permission and through the courtesy of: *Newscom:* Andre Jenny Stock Connection Worldwide, 4; *Alamy:* Ancient Art & Architecture Collection Ltd., 7; The Print Collector, 8; Mark J. Barrett, 9; Fresh Start Images, 12; Pat Canova, 16; Chris Mummery, 28; Classic Image, 30; *Landov:* K. Wothe/DPA, 14; *SuperStock:* Terrance Klassen/age fotostock, 17; Hemis.fr, 26; Prisma, 33; Barrett & MacKay/All Canada Photos, 37; *The Image Works:* David R. Frazier, 19; Mike Greenlar, 21; St Petersburg Times/Jim Damaske, 25; *Corbis:* Emily Anne Epstein, 22; *Getty Images:* Mark Suban/U.S. Air Force, 31; Frank Whitney/Iconica, 34; Hannes Magerstaedt, 40

Printed in the United States of America

Contents

One   People and Working Horses   5

Two   In Rural Areas   15

Three   In Cities and Towns   23

Four   In Government Service   29

Five   In Sports and Entertainment   35

Glossary   42

Find Out More   44

Index   46

One

People and Working Horses

Clip-clop, clip-clop. The sound of horses' hooves on the cobblestone driveway awaken the hotel guests. A team of horses has pulled a wagon filled with the day's supplies to the hotel. The sound of working horses is heard all day, every day on Mackinac Island in Michigan's part of Lake Huron. More than six hundred horses from seventeen different **breeds** work on the island. Cars and trucks have not been allowed there since 1898.

Horse-drawn wagons carry food, mail, luggage, and other goods from ferryboats. They deliver these goods to the island's stores, shops, restaurants, and hotels. Horse-drawn taxis and carriages take some visitors to and from their hotels and all around the island. Other visitors rent horses from one of the island's stables. They can also rent horse-drawn carriages to drive themselves. Then they explore the island on their own.

← Horse-drawn carriages are a common sight on Michigan's Mackinac Island. They take the place of cars and trucks, which are not permitted.

Bicycles are for rent, too, but working horses are the main source of transportation for people and goods on the island.

Into the early 1900s, working horses like the ones on Mackinac Island were part of everyday life. People throughout the world, especially in the Americas and Europe, depended on working horses. These animals helped farmers plow, seed, and harvest their fields. On the open range and on ranches, horses moved cowboys among herds of cattle. In cities, horses pulled wagons that people used to haul firefighting equipment, to deliver milk and ice, and to carry away garbage. During wars, horses carried soldiers as they charged across battlefields. How did horses become so important to people?

What Is a Working Horse?

Working horses provide labor that helps people with their jobs. Many working horses pull farm equipment, wagons, and carriages. Other working horses are ridden by cowboys on ranches, by police officers in cities, and by soldiers. Still others race or perform in rodeos, circuses, or movies. These horses provide entertainment and earn money for their riders, drivers, trainers, and owners. That is why this book includes them as working horses.

The First Working Horses

By six thousand years ago, people in Central Asia had **domesticated** horses. People milked the mares—adult female horses—and drank the milk. To add to their herds, people **bred** the mares to the stallions, or adult male horses. For food, the people would kill some stallions for their meat.

Little by little, men and women trained horses to do work. First, horses worked as pack animals, carrying loads. A horse could carry a much heavier load than a person could.

Next, people realized that horses could be trained for riding. **Archaeologists** have found horses' teeth that are 5,500 years old. The teeth show wear from bits. A bit is a metal bar that is placed in a horse's mouth. The bit is attached to reins. By pulling on the reins, a rider tells the horse to turn right or left or to stop.

This ancient Roman relief depicts a soldier with a packhorse.

After the wheel was invented about five thousand years ago, two-wheeled carts came into use. People harnessed horses to the carts. These horses were the world's first draft horses. This type of horse is used for pulling loaded wagons, plows, carriages, sleighs, or other objects. A draft horse can pull a heavily loaded wagon or cart more easily than a packhorse can carry a load of the same weight.

Ancient Egyptians utilized two-wheeled, horse-drawn carts during harvest seasons.

Shires are one of the largest and strongest breeds making them great workhorses.

Qualities of Working Horses

What qualities make horses such good workers? First, horses are smart. They can be trained to respond to human commands. They can also be trained to perform certain jobs or tasks. Horses have good long-term memories and seem able to form strong bonds with their human handlers.

Second, horses are strong. They are built to be powerful workers. Horses have deep, wide chests and muscular rear legs. This makes their bodies balanced and able to pull heavy loads. Large lungs and wide nostrils enable horses to take deep breaths. This means horses are well suited for long, slow, and heavy work. It also allows them to run with bursts of speed.

Third, because of the way they are built, horses can work for longer periods of time than other animals can. They can work all day and only need grass, hay, and water to keep them going. Horses need only about three hours of sleep a day. They lie down to sleep for short amounts of time but get most of their rest during several naps while standing.

Fourth, horses can do many kinds of work. They can pull a plow, a sled, a wagon, or a carriage. They can also carry riders over long distances. Finally, horses can move faster than other work animals can. They can also move at several different speeds. Horses have four natural **gaits**. They can **walk**, **trot**, **canter**, and **gallop**. At a walk, they average 4 miles per hour; at a trot, 8 miles per hour; at a canter, 10 to 17 miles per hour; and at a gallop, 25 to 30 miles per hour.

Many Breeds of Working Horses

During the past five thousand years, people have been **crossbreeding** horses. This means a stallion from one breed is mated with a mare from another breed. By crossbreeding, people have developed new breeds of horses with characteristics they want. In this way, some horses became bigger. Others became stronger. Still others became faster.

Different breeds of horses have performed different jobs. Belgians, Clydesdales, Percherons, and shires are some of the biggest and heaviest draft horses. They have worked farm fields and pulled heavily loaded wagons. Long ago, they carried knights in armor onto battlefields. Lighter, faster horses, such as mustangs and American quarter horses, became good at herding cattle. The fastest horses, such as **Thoroughbreds** and American **standardbreds**, became racehorses.

The Largest and the Smallest Working Horses

Shires are some of the largest draft horses. Since 1850, Sampson, a shire, has held the record as the world's largest horse. This English horse weighed 3,360 pounds. He stood 21.2 $^1/_2$ **hands** high, or 86.5 inches. A hand equals 4 inches—the average width of an adult's hand. Horses are measured in hands from the ground to their **withers**.

Shetland ponies weigh in on the other end of the scale. These small horses come from Scotland's Shetland Islands. Some Shetlands weigh only 170 pounds and are less than 10 hands (40 inches) high. Because they are so small, Shetlands are usually measured in inches instead of in hands.

Cyldesdales originated in Scotland. They were used in agriculture, for hauling coal, and for doing other heavy work.

People, Working Horses, and Machines

Horses took on more and more of the heavy work that people once did. Horsepower replaced manpower. During the 1800s and early 1900s, horses powered many machines. People even thought of horses as machines. Hitched to wheels and gears, horses ground grain in mills and lifted cranes at building sites. They pulled streetcars, fire rigs, and early railroad cars.

By the 1930s the horsepower of cars, trucks, railroads, tractors, and army tanks had replaced most working horses. In fact, the term **horsepower** compares the work done by today's machines to the work done by a horse. People are compared to horses, too. Sometimes people are called workhorses. That means they are hard workers and can be depended on to do a good job—just like a working horse.

In the 1970s two events caused working horses to become popular again. First, a movement to clean up the environment began. One way to do that was to use alternative transportation in order to reduce air pollution from gasoline-powered vehicles. Second, a shortage of gasoline occurred. That caused fuel prices to rise steeply and quickly. Later, in the early 2000s, the price of fuel increased sharply. Some farmers and police departments started using working horses again. Working horses were the perfect solution to the problems of air pollution and the high cost of fuel.

Two

In Rural Areas

Working horses often bring to mind rural areas, such as farms and ranches. Indeed, horses working on farms and ranches continue to help feed the world today. Sometimes horses work in forests and in the sea, too.

On Farms

Farms were some of the first places where people used horses. Today, horses continue to work on farms around the world. In some countries in central Europe, draft horses still do most of the plowing, planting, weeding, and harvesting.

In the United States, many farmers never stopped using draft horses on their farms. Today, thousands of farmers prefer to use horses rather than motorized machines. These farmers like the easy, quiet pace of horses.

← Working horses help farmers with heavy hauling.

Two horses pull a plow through a farmer's field.

Draft horses provide a smoother ride over the fields than do tractors. They also do not make the noise that tractors and other machines do. In addition, horses do not pack down the fields as much as tractors and other equipment do. Plus, horses can be harnessed to all the equipment that is needed to work a farm. That equipment includes plows, seeders, cultivators, harvesters, corn pickers, mowers, balers, and manure and fertilizer spreaders.

Draft horses such as Belgians, Clydesdales, Percherons, and shires are usually picked for farmwork. They are tall, strong horses. Their short backs, powerful hindquarters, and heavy bones make them perfect for pulling farm equipment. A team of draft horses can work about ten hours a day, walking at about 3 miles an hour.

Most farmers who use horses have small farms. The number of horses a farmer has depends on the size of the farm. Some farmers might have only two or three horses. Others might use teams of twelve to work their fields.

Most farms worked by horses have a variety of areas. In a farm's pastureland, the horses can graze on grass. Hay is grown in some fields. Horses hitched to various equipment help with all phases of growing hay.

Amish Farmers

In the United States, the Amish rely completely on horses to work their farms and to provide transportation. The religious beliefs of the Amish do not allow them to use electricity, cars, or other motorized machines. The largest Amish populations live in Indiana, Ohio, and Pennsylvania.

Belgians and Percherons are the draft horses that Amish farmers use most often. They use standardbreds to pull their black buggies along country roads and into nearby towns. Their standardbreds are often retired harness-racing horses.

After it is cut, much of the hay is set aside to feed the horses. Other fields are used to grow vegetables, corn, and oats. Manure produced by the horses is used to fertilize the fields.

Farmers use their horses for tasks other than working the fields. Some farmers earn extra money by hitching their teams to hay wagons and sleighs. In the fall, groups of people visit those farms for hayrides. In the winter, people enjoy sleigh rides through snow-covered fields.

On Ranches

Owners of many ranches continue to use cowboys on horseback to round up and herd cattle. Most of those ranches are in the United States, Canada, South America, Australia, and some parts of Europe. In Scotland, farmers on horseback sometimes round up sheep.

Many breeds of horses, such as Appaloosas, mustangs, paints, pintos, and quarter horses, work on U.S. ranches. All ranch horses must quickly obey the commands of their riders. Most cowboys in the United States prefer quarter horses. These horses are bred to run fast over short distances. Quarter horses got their name because they can sprint one-quarter of a mile in less than twenty-one seconds. Besides getting off to a quick start, quarter horses can change directions and stop quickly. These skills are needed to keep the cattle moving in the right direction. The quarter horses' skills also help cowboys to rope cattle and to separate certain cattle from the herd.

A ranch horse helps its rider round up cattle.

The main job of ranch horses is helping control cattle. That is why the horses are sometimes called cow ponies. In the spring, ranch horses help round up the calves on the open range for branding. In the fall, the horses help round up the cattle and herd them back to corrals or pens on the ranch. From there, the horses help separate the younger cattle from the older ones. The horses also help separate out some males and females.

Logging and Other Forest Work

Horses have worked in the forestry industry for many years. For a draft horse, a log is just something else to pull or to drag. After lumberjacks cut down and trim branches from trees, horses drag the heavy logs out of the forest. Then the logs are loaded onto trucks.

In areas where only a few trees are being cut down, horses are especially effective workers. They can walk along trails that are too narrow for trucks or tractors. In addition, horses are easier on the forest's floor. They do not pack down the dirt the way heavy trucks do. Horses also do not pollute the

19

Unusual Jobs for Working Horses

In the past, horses in rural areas worked underground and near water. From the 1800s until the 1990s, Shetland ponies worked in coal mines in England and Scotland. Miners built stables inside the mines. The Shetlands ate, slept, and worked underground. They pulled carts filled with coal out of the mines. The work of these small horses helped supply coal to heat homes and to run factories.

In the early 1800s in the United States, horses pulled barges along canals. Canals were dug to connect waterways. Barges carried grain, lumber, and finished goods on the canals. Horses walked next to the canals and pulled the barges to which they were hitched.

Horses also helped power ferryboats. These boats take people and goods from one side of a river or lake to the other side. In the 1800s some ferries were horse driven. A horse walked in place on a treadmill that was on the ferry's deck. The treadmill was attached to the ferry's paddle wheel, which turned as the horse walked.

clean forest air with exhaust fumes. Plus, their manure provides fertilizer that helps young trees and other forest plants grow.

Some farms have wooded areas. Each year, the farmers choose which trees they want to cut down. They use their draft horses to drag the logs out of the woods. Then the farmers might split the logs for firewood or trim the logs into boards to repair fences or farm buildings.

Horses are also useful on Christmas tree farms. A horse can pull a wagon stacked with cut trees from the field without disturbing the uncut trees. The width of the horse and wagon is less than that of a truck.

Horses are used to haul logs in heavily wooded areas.

In the Sea

For five hundred years, men have ridden horses into the North Sea to catch shrimp. Today, only a few Belgian shrimpers and their Brabant horses continue this work. Each shrimper trains his own horse. The horse and shrimper work together for many years. The men hitch nets behind their horses and ride out into the sea. The nets scoop up shrimp, other shellfish, and fish.

At one time, the shrimp caught this way were used to fertilize farm fields. Now, the shrimpers eat the shrimp or sell it to others to eat.

Three

In Cities and Towns

Horses work not only in rural areas, such as farms, ranches, forests, or seaside villages, but also in cities and towns. Some working horses carry police officers through city traffic. Others pull tourists or couples in fancy carriages.

Mounted Police Units

The first mounted police unit in the United States was formed in New York City in 1871. By the 1930s most police departments were using police cars rather than horses. In the 1970s several U.S. cities started using mounted police units again. By the early 2000s, about eighty-five cities had them. Today, cities in about thirty countries, including Australia, Canada, China, India, and Italy, have mounted police.

← A mounted police officer patrols Times Square in New York City.

Mounted police units have many benefits. One officer and horse can do the job of seven to ten officers on foot. Horses can carry the officers faster than the officers could travel on foot. Mounted police units can move through traffic more easily than a squad car can. Seated on horses,

The American Society for the Prevention of Cruelty to Animals

In the 1860s some people in New York City noticed that people were treating horses badly. Some drivers whipped or beat their horses to make them work harder. Stalls in some stables were dirty and cold. Many horses were not properly fed or cared for.

In 1866 in New York, Henry Bergh founded the American Society for the Prevention of Cruelty to Animals (ASPCA). At first, the group worked mainly to protect working horses. By the early 1900s, cars, trucks, and streetcars began to replace horses. The ASPCA then turned its attention to dogs and cats.

Today, the ASPCA continues to work for the protection of all kinds of animals, horses included. Now, it focuses on horses that are rented from riding stables and that pull carriages in cities. The ASPCA is also concerned about the living and working conditions of racehorses.

officers also can see above crowds. Mounted police units are sometimes called 10-foot cops.

Mounted units are also good at controlling large crowds at parades and sporting events. The horses' large bodies keep people from entering unsafe areas. Some cities even send mounted units into high-crime areas.

Some horses start training for police work shortly after they are born. Others are retired racehorses or farm horses. Those horses receive training for about three to six months before they begin mounted police duty. All police horses have to learn to walk through crowds and not to jump at loud noises.

The mounted officers go through special training, too. Each mounted officer rides the same horse every day. The officer feeds, saddles, and brushes the horse. The mounted officer and horse work as a team. Their partnership lasts for many years. Many mounted police officers ride Morgans or quarter horses, as well as Thoroughbreds, standard-breds, and other breeds.

This police officer has a special bond with his horse.

Horses have an average life span of twenty to twenty-five years. Most police horses retire before they reach twenty. They spend the rest of their years grazing in pastures. Police officers often visit their retired partners.

Horse-Drawn Carriages

Today, horse-drawn carriages are major attractions in some cities, such as New York, Chicago, and New Orleans. They are usually found in downtown areas or in large city parks. Horse-drawn car-riages must be licensed, just as taxicabs. They also must observe traffic laws, stop signs, and stoplights. Many cities and towns require

A couple enjoys a horse-drawn carriage ride through New York City's Central Park.

drivers to clean up after their horses. For safety as well as for a more pleasant drive, most horse-drawn carriages avoid the high-traffic times of the morning and early evening.

One horse usually pulls an open carriage, allowing passengers to view the city's sights. Draft horses are often chosen for this kind of carriage duty. Many drivers dress as carriage drivers did during the 1800s and early 1900s. They wear top hats and clothing from earlier times.

Horse-drawn carriages are also used for weddings and high school proms. A white carriage pulled by a gray horse often takes a bride and groom from the church to their wedding reception. Some people would

Working Horses Influence Language

Until the early 1900s, horses did an incredible amount of work for people. As machines replaced working horses, the new machines were often compared to horses. When the first locomotives chugged across the country, many people called them "iron horses." The first automobiles were sometimes called "horseless carriages."

Today, people who drive large trucks across the country are called "teamsters." The original teamsters drove teams of horses that pulled loaded wagons through and between cities.

say these horses are white, but they are actually gray. Rather than hiring a limousine for their proms, some teenagers now arrive at the big dance in a horse-drawn carriage. Horses pulling carriages for weddings and proms are sometimes decked out with bells and flowers.

A ride in a horse-drawn carriage adds elegance to special occasions. People who take these rides often compliment drivers on the smooth, leisurely pace. They like the quietness of the ride, too. Of course, they also admire the beauty of the horses.

Four

In Government Service

For thousands of years, governments used horses to keep the peace and to wage war. By the mid–1900s, Jeeps, tanks, trucks, and all-terrain vehicles (ATVs) had replaced horses on the battlefield. Military horses remained in use for special government ceremonies, however. Recently, some countries have started training soldiers to ride and to pack horses again.

Military Service

World War I (1914–1918) was the last war in which cavalry, or units of soldiers fighting on horseback, were heavily used. During World War II (1939–1945), the last U.S. cavalry charge took place in the Philippines in 1942. Now, cavalry units are made up of tanks and ATVs.

← A mounted Swedish Royal Guard and his horse during the changing-of-the-guard ceremony.

Since 2001 the U.S. Army and the U.S. Marine Corps have trained some troops to use horses. Soldiers and marines learn how to ride horses in mountainous areas. They also learn how to load equipment onto packhorses. Most of this training takes place in the mountains of California and Colorado.

World War I saw mounted combat between Russian and German cavalry.

Early Instructions about Military Horses

Xenophon (c. 431–c. 352 BCE) was a Greek general and a historian. He wrote *On the Cavalry Commander*. This is one of the earliest books on horsemanship in warfare. Xenophon gave instructions on how to mount a horse, to control its movements, and to fight on horseback. He said that riders should treat their horses with understanding, and they should never show anger when approaching a horse. Military units still follow Xenophon's instructions today.

The armies of Afghanistan, Austria, Germany, and Switzerland also have mounted units. They train in mountainous and heavily forested areas. Afghanistan's army uses Afghan ponies. They are much like the mustangs of the United States. The Austrians and Germans prefer Haflinger mountain horses. The Swiss use Freiberger Swiss mountain horses.

Ceremonial Horses

Military horses often appear in special government ceremonies. These horse units take part in retirement ceremonies, parades, and other military events. The horses wear special military gear, and soldiers who are part of the regular army ride them. Military horses are usually retired when they are about fifteen years old.

President Ronald Reagan's casket and caisson are pulled by three teams of horses.

In the United States, military horses play an important role in military and presidential funerals. In those funerals, the casket is carried on a caisson. A caisson is a wagon for carrying weapons and ammunition. It is pulled by three two-horse teams, plus a lead horse. The three horses on the left side of each team carry a rider.

The Riderless Horse

In presidential funerals and in some high-ranking military funerals, a riderless horse follows the caisson. A pair of boots faces backward in the stirrups. This signifies the leader's last look at his or her troops. The riderless horse is led by a soldier on foot.

The seventh horse, with its rider, walks to the left of the first team.

In London, England, a ceremony called Trooping the Colour takes place each June in honor of the queen's birthday. More than two hundred horses and their riders take part in this colorful event. The horses are part of the Household Cavalry Mounted Regiment, and the riders are members of the British Army. Today, the queen receives the royal salute while riding in a horse-drawn carriage. When she was younger, she received the salute while on horseback.

Military horses take part in other special royal family events. In 2011 the wedding procession of Prince William and his bride Catherine "Kate" Middleton included almost two hundred horses and riders from the Household Cavalry. Two teams of gray horses pulled the bridal carriage from Westminster Abbey to Buckingham Palace. The carriage did not

British soldiers and their horses take part in Trooping the Colour.

have a driver. Instead, soldiers rode the horses on the left side of each team. For protection, soldiers on black horses rode alongside and behind the carriage. Four other carriages with similar horses and riders followed the bridal carriage. They carried other members of the bridal party and members of the royal family.

Five

In Sports and Entertainment

Horses also work as athletes and entertainers. Their workplaces are race-courses, circus tents, arenas, and stadiums. Warhorses were the first to use many of these athletes' and entertainers' skills and moves.

At the Racetrack

Horses have been raced almost from the time they were first ridden and driven. Early riders galloped across fields to see whose horse would reach a certain point first. Harness racing is sometimes traced to ancient chariot races. Two-wheeled chariots pulled by teams of horses raised dust on racetracks in ancient Greece and Rome. Sharp curves at each end of the track made for exciting races.

← Racehorses and their jockeys speed toward the finish line at Saratoga Racetrack in New York.

Today, riders of racehorses are called jockeys. Most jockeys weigh about 100 pounds. They have to be light so their horses can run fast. Jockeys ride Thoroughbreds at a full-out gallop. During the gallop, all four of the horse's hooves are off the ground at the same time. Thoroughbreds' long, slender legs give them a long stride. Thoroughbreds can reach speeds of up to 40 miles per hour.

Every spring, the best three-year-old Thoroughbreds compete for the Triple Crown. They try to win three races—the Kentucky Derby, the Preakness Stakes in Maryland, and the Belmont Stakes in New York. In 1978, Affirmed became the last horse to win the Triple Crown.

In a harness race, standardbred horses pull a **sulky**—a small, low, two-wheeled cart with a seat for a driver. Standardbreds have shorter

The Origin of Thoroughbreds

All Thoroughbreds are descended from one of three Arabian stallions. In the 1600s and 1700s, those three horses were brought to England from the Middle East. Bedouins in the deserts of the Middle East had bred the horses' ancestors for speed. Bedouins have a saying, "God created the Thoroughbred from a handful of wind." That, they say, is why Thoroughbreds can run so fast.

Standardbred horses pull sulkies when they race.

legs than Thoroughbreds do, but their backs are longer. They also have heavier bones.

The standardbred was so named because it could trot or pace one mile in a standard time of no longer than 2.4 minutes. A harness race is one mile long. Today, most standardbreds can finish a harness race in less than two minutes.

Standardbreds are the fastest pacing and trotting horses. A **pacer** runs at a pace. This means that both legs on the same side are off the ground at the same time. A **trotter** runs at a trot. This means that the diagonal front and back legs are off the ground at the same time. If a horse breaks into a gallop during a harness race, the horse is disqualified.

Thoroughbreds and jockeys, as well as standardbreds and drivers, compete to win prize money for the horses' owners. This is why Thoroughbreds and standardbreds are working horses. The money they win pays for their feed and equipment. It also helps pay their jockeys, drivers, and trainers.

At the Rodeo

Rodeos are popular in the United States and Canada. Every summer, the Calgary Stampede is held in Calgary, Alberta, in Canada. In late fall, the National Finals Rodeo (NFR) takes place in Las Vegas, Nevada. Thousands of people attend these rodeo competitions and cheer on their favorite cowboys and cowgirls.

The First Rodeo

In 1882 Buffalo Bill Cody held the first rodeo in North Platte, Nebraska. It was called Buffalo Bill's Wild West. Cody hired cowboys to entertain the public. They performed in outdoor rings as well as in indoor arenas. The cowboys roped cows and rode bulls and bucking broncos (untamed mustangs). Cody took his show to cities throughout the United States and to other countries. Audiences saw what cowboys and their horses did during roundups and cattle drives.

During rodeos, cowboys show off their roping and riding skills. They also put their horses to the test. Cowboys on horseback compete to see how quickly they can rope and tie a calf or steer. Their horses help them by changing directions and stopping quickly when the calf or steer has been roped. Cowboys show off their horses' other skills, too. They have them make sliding stops, back up, and walk sideways.

Rodeo cowgirls specialize in barrel races. While riding at a gallop, they guide their horses around a series of barrels. The object of this contest is to see who can complete the series the fastest, without knocking over a barrel.

At the Circus

The first circus horses performed at circuses in ancient Rome. Today, circus horses and their riders do many of the same tricks as they did then. During performances, horses follow the commands of their trainers. These horses jump through hoops and over high bars. They also walk on their back legs.

Some circus horses gallop around the ring with performers riding bareback (without a saddle). Other circus horses run with one or more performers standing on them bareback. Performers often do their own tricks, such as somersaults or ballet steps, on the backs of moving horses.

The main breeds of circus horses are Andalusians, Arabians, and Lipizzaners. Lipizzaner stallions are known for a special performance called Airs above the Ground. The airs are leaps and jumps in which the horse has two or four feet off the ground at the same time. The most famous of the Lipizzaners' moves is the capriole. The horse leaps into the air with all four hooves several feet off the ground. When he is in midair, he draws his front legs under his chest and kicks out with his hind legs.

Some horses are trained to work in the circus.

Trainers use special tools to teach circus horses new tricks. One tool is a clicker. Another tool is the lunge whip. The sounds that the clicker and long-handled whip make tell the horses what to perform. The trainers do not hit the horses with the whips.

In Movies, on Television, and in Theaters

Horses can also be trained to act. They learn to do certain moves or tricks. Some of these moves are backing up, bowing, lying down, nodding, pawing the ground, standing on their hind legs, and stepping sideways. Trainers teach these actors to recognize special cues or signals so they know when to make their moves.

Horses that work as actors begin training almost from birth. They have to get used to working with people. They cannot be afraid of the sounds and lights used when making movies and television shows. Horses that take part in battle scenes must be able to work with other horses as well as their riders. In that way, they can all move in the right direction at the same time.

Recently, people have built several theaters for horse performances. Medieval Times Dinner & Tournament presents jousting tournaments. Horses and riders wear costumes like the ones that knights and their mounts wore in the Middle Ages. Andalusians, Friesians, quarter horses, and Menorcans perform in these shows. They begin training at only a few months old. By four years of age, they start performing. They work for only a few years. Then they retire to the Medieval Times ranch in Texas.

There are about 9.2 million horses in the United States today. About 28 percent of them are working horses. Many of them help farmers, ranchers, and loggers. Some work with police officers and soldiers. Other working horses pull carriages. Still others race or perform in circuses, rodeos, movies, television shows, and theaters. Owners, trainers, drivers, and riders do their best to take good care of their working horses. They continue the close relationships among people, horses, and work that began thousands of years ago.

Glossary

archaeologists Scientists who research the past by studying the remains of past human activity.

bred Mated male and female animals in order to produce more of the same type of animal.

breeds Groups of animals with similar characteristics.

canter To move at the three-beat gait of a horse that is typically faster than a trot but slower than a gallop.

crossbreeding Mating horses of different types in order to develop a new type of horse.

domesticated Adapted a type of animal through breeding so that it can live with or be used by people.

gaits Ways of moving on two or four legs.

gallop To move at the fastest speed of a horse.

hand Measurement used to express the height of a horse from the ground to its withers; 1 hand equals 4 inches.

horsepower The power that a horse exerts in pulling.

pacer   A harness-racing horse that runs at a gait called a pace, with both legs on the same side of its body off the ground at the same time.

standardbreds   Members of a breed of trotting and pacing horses used especially in harness racing.

sulky   A low, lightweight, two-wheeled harness-racing vehicle with a small seat for the driver.

Thoroughbreds   A racehorse that traces its ancestors to one of three founding sires.

trot   To move at the two-beat gait of a horse that is between a walk and a canter, during which the diagonal front and rear legs are off the ground at the same time.

trotter   A harness-racing horse that moves at a trot (see above).

walk   To move at a horse's slowest gait.

withers   The area between the neck and back of the horse, just beyond the end of the mane.

Find Out More

Books

Apte, Sunita. *Police Horses*. New York: Bearport Publishing Company, 2007.

Edwards, Elwyn Hartley. *The Encyclopedia of the Horse*. New York: Dorling Kindersley, 2008.

Sandler, Michael. *Military Horses*. New York: Bearport Publishing Company, 2007.

DVDs

The Farmer and the Horse. Hundred Year Films, 2010.

The Working Shire Horse. Travel Video Store, 2010.

 44

Websites

Breeds of Livestock: Horses

www.ansi.okstate.edu/breeds/horses
Just about every horse breed in the world is given a page describing its origin, history, and main uses.

The Harness Horse Youth Foundation

www.hhyf.org
Learn everything you want to know about harness racing, from how to become a driver through internships and scholarships to information about famous harness horses.

Index

Page numbers in **boldface** are illustrations.

acting work, 40–41
American Society for the Prevention of Cruelty to Animals (ASPCA), 24
Amish farmers, 17, **17**
archaeologists, 7

breeds and breeding, 5, 7, 10–11
Buffalo Bill, 38

caisson, 31, **31**
canal work, 20
canter, 10
carts, two-wheeled, 8, **8**, 35
ceremonial horses, **28**, **31**, 31–33
chariot racing, 35
circus, 39–40, **40**
Clydesdales, 11, **12**, 16
crossbreeding, 10–11, 42

definition, working horse, 6
domesticated, 7
draft horses, 8, **8**, **9**, **12**, 16

environmental concerns, 13, 19–21

farms, 6, **14**, 15–18, **16**
ferryboats, 20
firefighting, 6
forest work, 19–21, **21**
funerals, 31, 32

gaits, 10
gallop, 10
government service, **28**, 29–33, **30**, **31**, **33**

hand, 11
harness racing, 35, 36–37, **37**
hayrides, 18
herding, 6, 18–19, **19**
history, working horses, 7–8
horse-drawn wagons/carriages, **4**, 5, **26**, 26–27
horseless carriages, 27
horsepower, 13
Household Cavalry Mounted Regiment, 32–33, **33**

intelligence, 9
iron horses, 27

jockeys, 36

language, influence of horses, 27
life span of horses, 25
Lipizzaner stallions, 39–40
logging, 19–21, **21**

Mackinac Island, **4**, 5–6
Medieval Times Dinner &
    Tournament, 41
military service, 6, **28**, 29–33,
    30, **31**, **33**
mining, 20

pacer, 37
packhorses, 7, **7**, 8
police work, **22**, 23–25, **25**
pollution, 13, 19–20
population of horses, 41

qualities of working horses, 9–10

racehorses, **34**, 35–38, **37**
ranch work, 18–19, **19**
riding, 7

rodeos, 38–39

Shetland ponies, 11, 20
shires, **9**, 11, 16
shrimpers, 21
sleigh rides, 18
sports and entertainment, **34**,
    35–41, **37**, **40**
standardbreds, 11, 36–38, **37**
strength and stamina, 9–10
sulky, 36, **37**
Swedish Royal Guard, **28**

teamsters, 27
Thoroughbreds, 11, 36, 38
Trooping the Colour, 32, **33**
trot/trotter, 10, 37
walk, 10
withers, 11
workhorses, 13

Xenophon (Greek general/
    historian), 30

About the Author

Patricia K. Kummer was once a horse-crazy kid. She collected porcelain horses, read every book about horses that she could find, and went horseback riding every once in a while. She now enjoys going to Thoroughbred and harness races. During a recent visit to Mackinac Island, she rode in and saw much horse-drawn equipment.

Kummer has a BA and an MA in history and has taught middle-school social studies. She has written more than sixty books about states, countries, inventions, and other topics. Other books that she has written are *Minnesota* and *Mississippi* in the Celebrate the States series, *The Great Barrier Reef* and *The Great Lakes* in the Nature's Wonders series, and *The Food of Thailand* in the Flavors of the World series.